Teach Your Child to Read

300 Short Easy Sentences

English - Croatian

Name

I Can...

- [ ] read the 1st sentence.
- [ ] read the 2nd sentence.
- [ ] make a sentence from a picture.
- [ ] color a picture.
- [ ] Draw a picture.

The frog is going to a party.

Žaba ide na zabavu.

The happy frog is wearing a green hat.

Sretna žaba nosi zeleni šešir.

Name

I Can...

- [ ] read the 1st sentence.
- [ ] read the 2nd sentence.
- [ ] make a sentence from a picture.
- [ ] color a picture.
- [ ] Draw a picture.

Owl likes to read big books.

Sova voli čitati velike knjige.

A smart owl is reading an alphabet book.

Pametna sova čita knjigu abeceda.

3

I Can...

- [ ] read the 1st sentence.
- [ ] read the 2nd sentence.
- [ ] make a sentence from a picture.
- [ ] color a picture.
- [ ] Draw a picture.

Come on! The ice cream truck is here!

Dođi! Kamion sladoleda je ovdje!

He is driving a big icecream truck.

Vozi veliki kamion sladoleda.

Name

I Can...

- [ ] read the 1st sentence.
- [ ] read the 2nd sentence.
- [ ] make a sentence from a picture.
- [ ] color a picture.
- [ ] Draw a picture.

Dragons are very friendly and have scales on their backs.

Zmajevi su vrlo prijateljski raspoloženi i imaju vage na leđima.

The dragon is waving his hand.

Zmaj mahne rukom.

Name

I Can...

- [ ] read the 1st sentence.
- [ ] read the 2nd sentence.
- [ ] make a sentence from a picture.
- [ ] color a picture.
- [ ] Draw a picture.

This ram lives in the farmhouse.

Ovaj ovna živi u seoskoj kući.

Ram has a large horn and fluffy wool.

Ram ima veliki rog i lepršavu vunu.

Name

I Can...

- [ ] read the 1st sentence.
- [ ] read the 2nd sentence.
- [ ] make a sentence from a picture.
- [ ] color a picture.
- [ ] Draw a picture.

The bunny likes to eat carrots.

Zeko voli jesti mrkvu.

Rabbit thinks that the juicy orange carrot looks yummy.

Rabbit misli da sočna narančasta mrkva izgleda ukusno.

Name

The clown likes to give out balloons to little kids.

Klovn voli djeci davati balone.

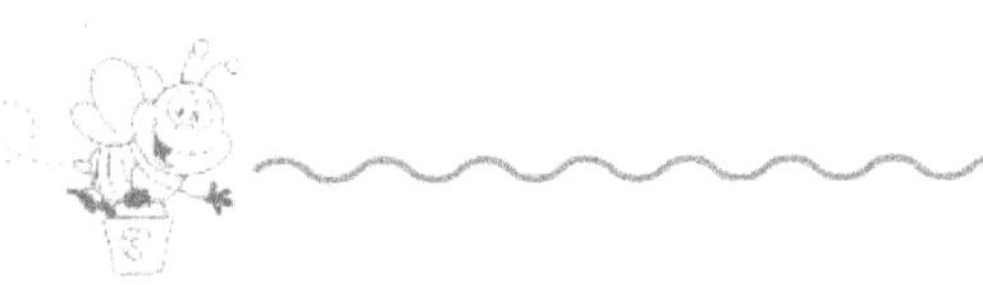

Funny, Mr. Clown is giving away colorful balloons.

Smiješno, g. Clown poklanja šarene balone.

Name

I Can...

- ☐ read the 1st sentence.
- ☐ read the 2nd sentence.
- ☐ make a sentence from a picture.
- ☐ color a picture.
- ☐ Draw a picture.

The clown is juggling balls for his performance.

Klovn žonglira lopticama za svoj nastup.

Talented, Mr. Clown is juggling five red balls.

Talentiran, gospodin Clown žonglira s pet crvenih kugli.

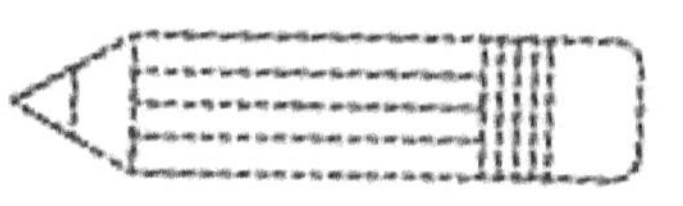

Name

I Can...

- ☐ read the 1st sentence.
- ☐ read the 2nd sentence.
- ☐ make a sentence from a picture.
- ☐ color a picture.
- ☐ Draw a picture.

The Easter Bunny is going to give out chocolate eggs.

Uskršnji zec će podijeliti čokoladna jaja.

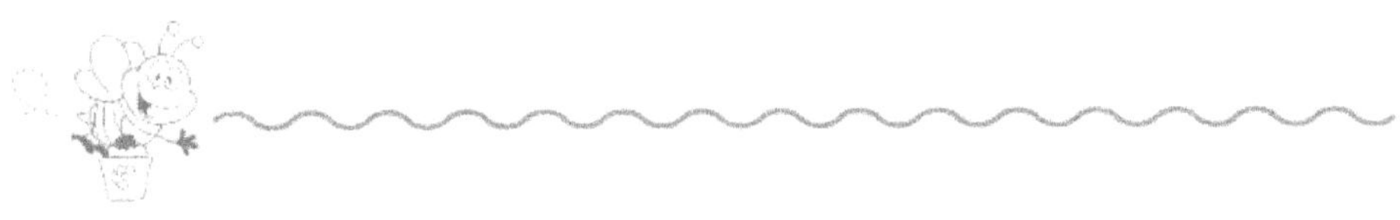

The rabbit goes out to buy more orange carrots.

Zec izlazi kupiti više narančaste mrkve.

Name

10

The pencil is drawing a zig-zag line.

Olovkom se crta cik-cak linija.

The Pencil is saying hello to you.

Olovka vas pozdravlja.

Name 

I Can...

- [ ] read the 1st sentence.
- [ ] read the 2nd sentence.
- [ ] make a sentence from a picture.
- [ ] color a picture.
- [ ] Draw a picture.

The pencil put on a big smile and went to work.

Olovka je navukla veliki osmijeh i krenula na posao.

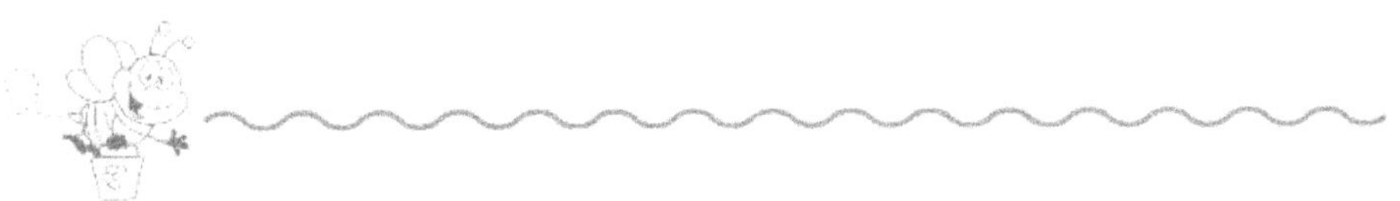

The Pencil is leaving to go on a long relaxing vacation.

Olovka odlazi na dugi opuštajući odmor.

Name

I Can...

- [ ] read the 1st sentence.
- [ ] read the 2nd sentence.
- [ ] make a sentence from a picture.
- [ ] color a picture.
- [ ] Draw a picture.

This snowman is my friend, and he is a helper of Santa.

Ovaj snjegović je moj prijatelj, a on je Djed Božićnjak.

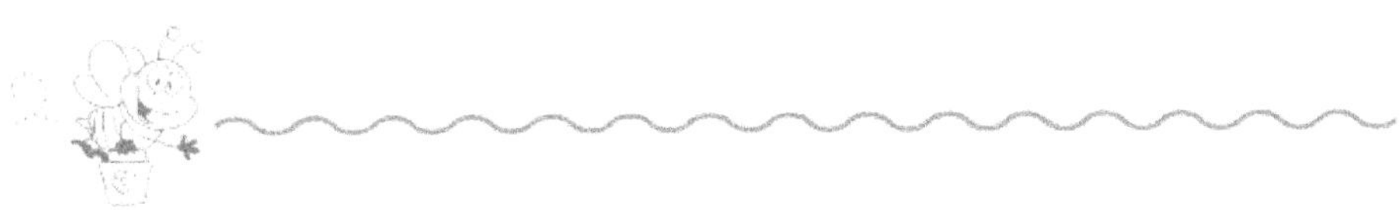

Mr. Snowman is celebrating Christmas by the decorated tree.

Gospodin Snjegović slavi Božić po ukrašenom drvcu.

I Can...

- [ ] read the 1st sentence.
- [ ] read the 2nd sentence.
- [ ] make a sentence from a picture.
- [ ] color a picture.
- [ ] Draw a picture.

The octopus is working as a chef and serving food.

Hobotnica radi kao kuhar i poslužuje hranu.

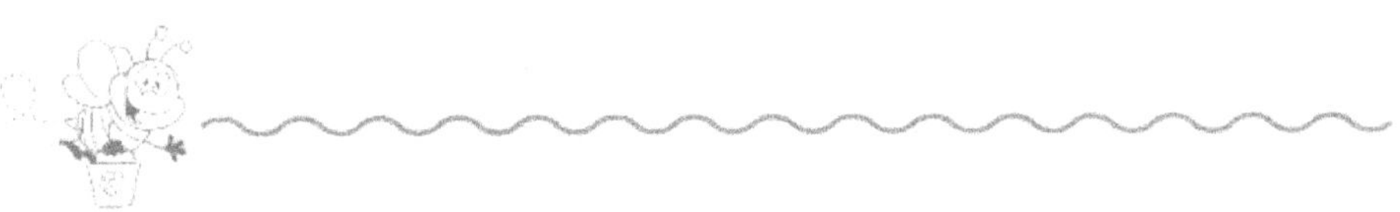

Chef Octopus is serving a delicious turkey dinner.

Chef Octopus poslužuje ukusnu večeru s puretinom.

Name

I Can...

- [ ] read the 1st sentence.
- [ ] read the 2nd sentence.
- [ ] make a sentence from a picture.
- [ ] color a picture.
- [ ] Draw a picture.

Santa is happy.

Djed Mraz je sretan.

Santa Claus is giving extraordinary presents to excited kids.

Djed Mraz daje izvanredne poklone uzbuđenoj djeci.

Name

I Can...

- read the 1st sentence.
- read the 2nd sentence.
- make a sentence from a picture.
- color a picture.
- Draw a picture.

The bear likes to eat sweets.

Medvjed voli jesti slatkiše.

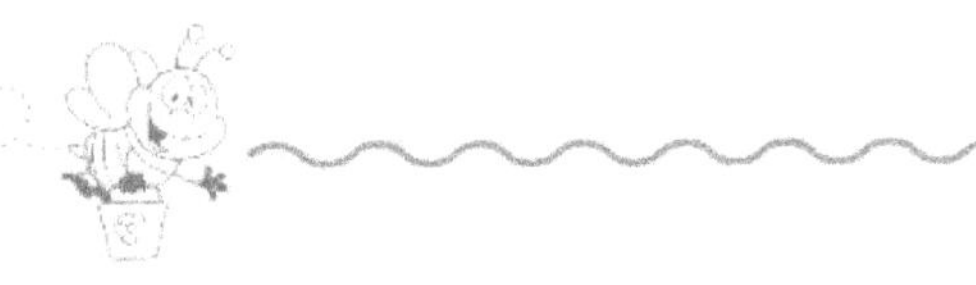

Teddy is licking a red and white candy cane.

Teddy liže kantu s crvenim i bijelim bombonima.

Name

I Can...

- [ ] read the 1st sentence.
- [ ] read the 2nd sentence.
- [ ] make a sentence from a picture.
- [ ] color a picture.
- [ ] Draw a picture.

The book has a wand.

Knjiga ima štapić.

The cereal box got a magician set for Christmas.

Kutija žitarica dobila je čarobnjački set za Božić.

Name

I Can...

- [ ] read the 1st sentence.
- [ ] read the 2nd sentence.
- [ ] make a sentence from a picture.
- [ ] color a picture.
- [ ] Draw a picture.

The bear has a present.

Medvjed ima poklon.

Happy Teddy is opening his box of presents from Santa.

Sretan Teddy otvara svoju Dječču kutiju s poklonima.

Name

I Can...

- [ ] read the 1st sentence.
- [ ] read the 2nd sentence.
- [ ] make a sentence from a picture.
- [ ] color a picture.
- [ ] Draw a picture.

Santa is going to give out presents.

Djed Mraz će podijeliti poklone.

Santa is lugging a large brown bag of gifts to his sley.

Djed Mraz ulepi veliku smeđu vrećicu s poklonima svome sleju.

Name

I made a snowman.

Napravio sam snjegovića.

Mr. Snowman is holding a broom and saying goodbye.

Gospodin Snowman drži metlu i pozdravlja se.

Name

I Can...

- [ ] read the 1st sentence.
- [ ] read the 2nd sentence.
- [ ] make a sentence from a picture.
- [ ] color a picture.
- [ ] Draw a picture.

The parrot is colorful.

Papiga je šarena.

The green parrot came from the forest to the zoo.

Zelena papiga došla je iz šume u zoološki vrt.

Name

I Can...

- [ ] read the 1st sentence.
- [ ] read the 2nd sentence.
- [ ] make a sentence from a picture.
- [ ] color a picture.
- [ ] Draw a picture.

There are a lot of animals.

Ima puno životinja.

The animals are happy being together again.

Životinje su sretne što su ponovno zajedno.

Name

I Can...

- [ ] read the 1st sentence.
- [ ] read the 2nd sentence.
- [ ] make a sentence from a picture.
- [ ] color a picture.
- [ ] Draw a picture.

The man is wearing a belt.

Čovjek nosi kaiš.

The carpenter is fixing something.

Stolar nešto popravlja.

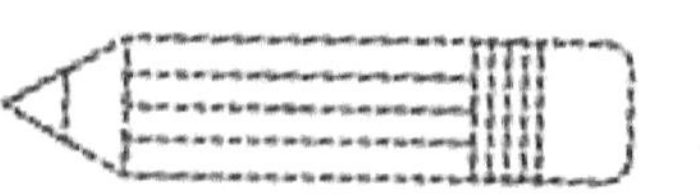

I Can...

- [ ] read the 1st sentence.
- [ ] read the 2nd sentence.
- [ ] make a sentence from a picture.
- [ ] color a picture.
- [ ] Draw a picture.

The rabbit is very young.

Zec je vrlo mlad.

The magician plays a trick.

Čarobnjak igra trik.

Name ____________________

I Can...

- ☐ read the 1st sentence.
- ☐ read the 2nd sentence.
- ☐ make a sentence from a picture.
- ☐ color a picture.
- ☐ Draw a picture.

He has a potion.

Ima napitak.

The scientist is making a potion.

Znanstvenica pravi napitak.

Name

I Can...

- [ ] read the 1st sentence.
- [ ] read the 2nd sentence.
- [ ] make a sentence from a picture.
- [ ] color a picture.
- [ ] Draw a picture.

He is wearing sunglasses.

Nosi sunčane naočale.

The policeman is mad.

Policajac je bijesan.

Name

I Can...

- [ ] read the 1st sentence.
- [ ] read the 2nd sentence.
- [ ] make a sentence from a picture.
- [ ] color a picture.
- [ ] Draw a picture.

He has a bucket of paint.

Ima kantu boje.

He likes to paint.

Voli slikati.

Name

I Can...

- [ ] read the 1st sentence.
- [ ] read the 2nd sentence.
- [ ] make a sentence from a picture.
- [ ] color a picture.
- [ ] Draw a picture.

The man has a hat.

Čovjek ima šešir.

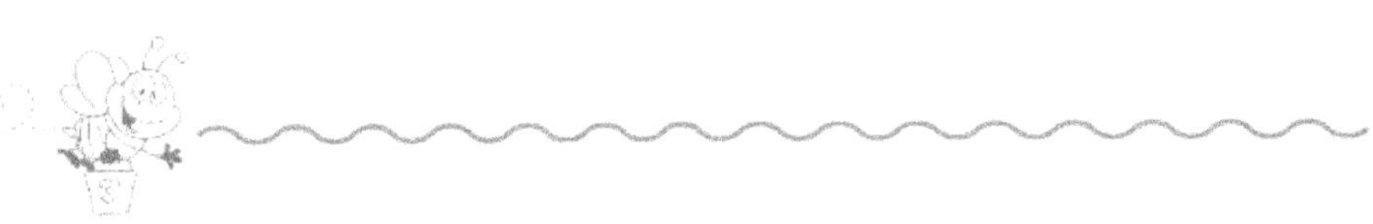

The postman is giving out the mail in the early morning.

Poštar rano ujutro odaje poštu.

I Can...

- [ ] read the 1st sentence.
- [ ] read the 2nd sentence.
- [ ] make a sentence from a picture.
- [ ] color a picture.
- [ ] Draw a picture.

He has a walkie talkie.

Ima voki-toki.

He is going to work with his suitcase.

On će raditi sa svojim kovčegom.

Name

I Can...

- [ ] read the 1st sentence.
- [ ] read the 2nd sentence.
- [ ] make a sentence from a picture.
- [ ] color a picture.
- [ ] Draw a picture.

He is sleepy.

Zaspao je.

The delivery man sent us a package.

Dostavljač nam je poslao paket.

Name

I Can...

- [ ] read the 1st sentence.
- [ ] read the 2nd sentence.
- [ ] make a sentence from a picture.
- [ ] color a picture.
- [ ] Draw a picture.

He is wearing a bowtie.

Nosi bowtie.

The waiter is serving juice.

Konobar poslužuje sok.

Name

I Can...

- ☐ read the 1st sentence.
- ☐ read the 2nd sentence.
- ☐ make a sentence from a picture.
- ☐ color a picture.
- ☐ Draw a picture.

He has a suitcase.

Ima kofer.

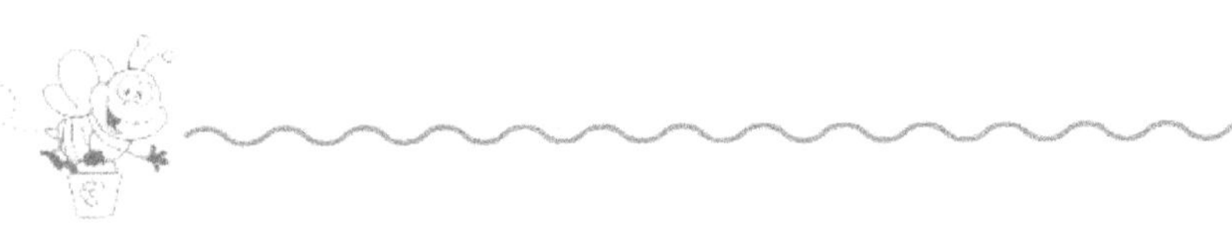

The engineer is holding a wrench.

Inženjer drži ključ.

Name

I Can...

- [ ] read the 1st sentence.
- [ ] read the 2nd sentence.
- [ ] make a sentence from a picture.
- [ ] color a picture.
- [ ] Draw a picture.

The chef has a napkin.

Kuhar ima ubrus.

The chef serves delicious-looking food.

Kuhar poslužuje ukusnu hranu.

Name

I Can...

- [ ] read the 1st sentence.
- [ ] read the 2nd sentence.
- [ ] make a sentence from a picture.
- [ ] color a picture.
- [ ] Draw a picture.

The rooster has a big beak.

Pijetao ima veliki kljun.

The chicken is saying hello to us.

Pile nas pozdravlja.

Name

I Can...

- [ ] read the 1st sentence.
- [ ] read the 2nd sentence.
- [ ] make a sentence from a picture.
- [ ] color a picture.
- [ ] Draw a picture.

The bird is small.

Ptica je mala.

The chick is on the telephone talking with his friend.

Pilić telefonom razgovara sa svojim prijateljem.

Name

I Can...

- [ ] read the 1st sentence.
- [ ] read the 2nd sentence.
- [ ] make a sentence from a picture.
- [ ] color a picture.
- [ ] Draw a picture.

That is my ring.

To je moj prsten.

That is a beautiful ring.

To je prekrasan prsten.

Name

I Can...

- [ ] read the 1st sentence.
- [ ] read the 2nd sentence.
- [ ] make a sentence from a picture.
- [ ] color a picture.
- [ ] Draw a picture.

The duck has three eggs.

Patka ima tri jaja.

The duck has a big nose.

Patka ima veliki nos.

Name

I Can...

- ☐ read the 1st sentence.
- ☐ read the 2nd sentence.
- ☐ make a sentence from a picture.
- ☐ color a picture.
- ☐ Draw a picture.

The swan is beautiful.

Labud je lijep.

The graceful swan is striding through the water.

Graciozni labud kreće kroz vodu.

Name

I Can...

- [ ] read the 1st sentence.
- [ ] read the 2nd sentence.
- [ ] make a sentence from a picture.
- [ ] color a picture.
- [ ] Draw a picture.

The girl is wearing a dress.

Djevojčica nosi haljinu.

The maid is cleaning our room.

Sluškinja čisti našu sobu.

Name

I Can...

- [ ] read the 1st sentence.
- [ ] read the 2nd sentence.
- [ ] make a sentence from a picture.
- [ ] color a picture.
- [ ] Draw a picture.

The boy is running.

Dječak bježi.

The little boy was running.

Mali je trčao.

Name 

I Can...

- [ ] read the 1st sentence.
- [ ] read the 2nd sentence.
- [ ] make a sentence from a picture.
- [ ] color a picture.
- [ ] Draw a picture.

He is a musician.

Glazbenik je.

He is playing a lively tune on his flute.

Svira živu melodiju na svojoj flauti.

Name

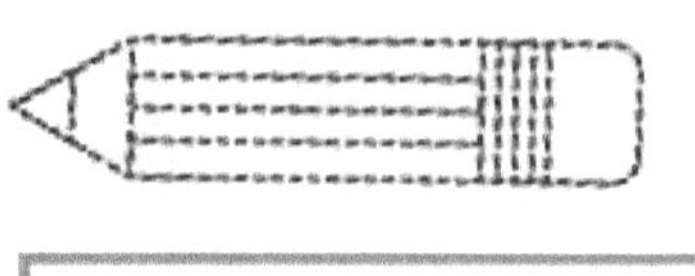

I Can...

- [ ] read the 1st sentence.
- [ ] read the 2nd sentence.
- [ ] make a sentence from a picture.
- [ ] color a picture.
- [ ] Draw a picture.

He looks joyful.

Izgleda radosno.

That boy works in a band and plays the drum.

Dječak radi u bendu i svira bubanj.

Name

I Can...

- [ ] read the 1st sentence.
- [ ] read the 2nd sentence.
- [ ] make a sentence from a picture.
- [ ] color a picture.
- [ ] Draw a picture.

The dinosaur is a rock star.

Dinosaur je rock zvijezda.

The dragon is playing the guitar.

Zmaj svira gitaru.

Name

I Can...

- [ ] read the 1st sentence.
- [ ] read the 2nd sentence.
- [ ] make a sentence from a picture.
- [ ] color a picture.
- [ ] Draw a picture.

The nurse helps the doctor.

Sestra pomaže liječniku.

~~~~~~

The nurse looks scary, holding a syringe.

Sestra izgleda zastrašujuće, držeći špricu.
~~~~~~

Name

I Can...

- [ ] read the 1st sentence.
- [ ] read the 2nd sentence.
- [ ] make a sentence from a picture.
- [ ] color a picture.
- [ ] Draw a picture.

She is wearing a crown.

Nosi vijenac.

The queen bee has a beautiful wand.

Kraljica pčela ima prekrasan štapić.

Name

I Can...

- [ ] read the 1st sentence.
- [ ] read the 2nd sentence.
- [ ] make a sentence from a picture.
- [ ] color a picture.
- [ ] Draw a picture.

It is orange and black.

Narančasta je i crna.

The tiger is wearing a bow on its neck.

Tigar nosi luk na vratu.

Name

I Can...

- [ ] read the 1st sentence.
- [ ] read the 2nd sentence.
- [ ] make a sentence from a picture.
- [ ] color a picture.
- [ ] Draw a picture.

The boy is carrying a lot of books.

Dječak nosi puno knjiga.

The boy is carrying so many books!

Dječak nosi toliko knjiga!

Name

I Can...

- [ ] read the 1st sentence.
- [ ] read the 2nd sentence.
- [ ] make a sentence from a picture.
- [ ] color a picture.
- [ ] Draw a picture.

The pizza looks delicious.

Pizza izgleda ukusno.

The waiter is serving steaming hot pizza.

Konobar poslužuje kuhanje vruće pizze.

Name

I Can...

- [ ] read the 1st sentence.
- [ ] read the 2nd sentence.
- [ ] make a sentence from a picture.
- [ ] color a picture.
- [ ] Draw a picture.

That is my dad's computer.

To je računalo mog oca.

My dad works on the computer.

Moj otac radi za računalom.

Name

I Can...

- [ ] read the 1st sentence.
- [ ] read the 2nd sentence.
- [ ] make a sentence from a picture.
- [ ] color a picture.
- [ ] Draw a picture.

The farmer has a beard.

Poljoprivrednik ima bradu.

The gardener is going to plant flowers

Vrtlar će saditi cvijeće

Name

I Can...

- [ ] read the 1st sentence.
- [ ] read the 2nd sentence.
- [ ] make a sentence from a picture.
- [ ] color a picture.
- [ ] Draw a picture.

The strawberry is red.

Jagoda je crvena.

I love to drink strawberry juice.

Obožavam piti sok od jagoda.

Name _______________________

I Can...

- ☐ read the 1st sentence.
- ☐ read the 2nd sentence.
- ☐ make a sentence from a picture.
- ☐ color a picture.
- ☐ Draw a picture.

The magician has a wand.

Čarobnjak ima štapić.

The wizard likes to work with magic.

Čarobnjak voli raditi s magijom.

Name 

I Can...

- [ ] read the 1st sentence.
- [ ] read the 2nd sentence.
- [ ] make a sentence from a picture.
- [ ] color a picture.
- [ ] Draw a picture.

Reindeer has a scarf.

Rena ima šal.

Santa gave reindeer a big present.

Djed Mraz poklonio je jelenima veliki poklon.

Name

I Can...

- [ ] read the 1st sentence.
- [ ] read the 2nd sentence.
- [ ] make a sentence from a picture.
- [ ] color a picture.
- [ ] Draw a picture.

I have a lot of pencils.

Imam puno olovaka.

I have a lot of brushes and pencils.

Imam puno četkica i olovaka.

I Can...

- [ ] read the 1st sentence.
- [ ] read the 2nd sentence.
- [ ] make a sentence from a picture.
- [ ] color a picture.
- [ ] Draw a picture.

Santa is fat.

Djed Mraz je debeo.

Santa is having fun.

Djed Mraz se zabavlja.

Name

I Can...

- [ ] read the 1st sentence.
- [ ] read the 2nd sentence.
- [ ] make a sentence from a picture.
- [ ] color a picture.
- [ ] Draw a picture.

I have one nose.

Imam jedan nos.

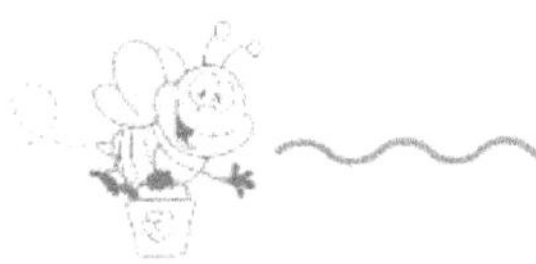

The one is saying its name.

Ona izgovara svoje ime.

Name

I Can...

- [ ] read the 1st sentence.
- [ ] read the 2nd sentence.
- [ ] make a sentence from a picture.
- [ ] color a picture.
- [ ] Draw a picture.

I have two ears.

Imam dva uha.

The number "two" is holding up bunny ears.

Broj "dva" drži gore zeko uši.

Name

I Can...

- [ ] read the 1st sentence.
- [ ] read the 2nd sentence.
- [ ] make a sentence from a picture.
- [ ] color a picture.
- [ ] Draw a picture.

I have three buttons on my dress.

Imam tri gumba na haljini.

The number "three" is saying you got 3 out of 3.

Broj "tri" govori da ste dobili 3 od 3.

Name

I Can...

- [ ] read the 1st sentence.
- [ ] read the 2nd sentence.
- [ ] make a sentence from a picture.
- [ ] color a picture.
- [ ] Draw a picture.

I have 0 tails.

Imam 0 repova.

The number "zero" is saying, Ok.

Broj "nula" kaže: U redu.

Name

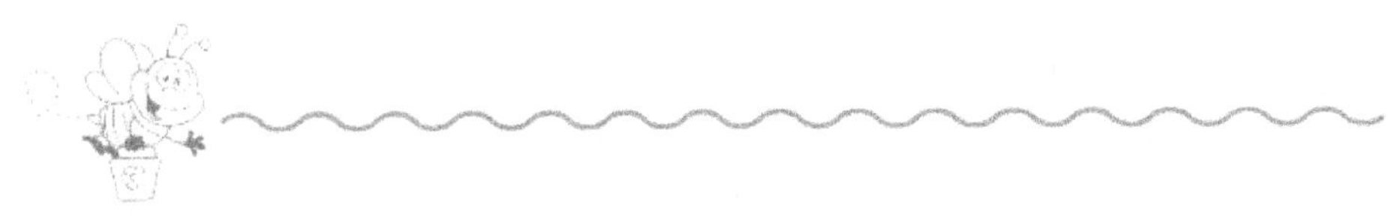

I Can...

- [ ] read the 1st sentence.
- [ ] read the 2nd sentence.
- [ ] make a sentence from a picture.
- [ ] color a picture.
- [ ] Draw a picture.

I have five fingers on 1 of my hands.

Na 1 ruku imam pet prstiju.

The number "five" is trying to give you a high five.

Broj "pet" pokušava vam dati visoku peticu.

Name

I Can...

- [ ] read the 1st sentence.
- [ ] read the 2nd sentence.
- [ ] make a sentence from a picture.
- [ ] color a picture.
- [ ] Draw a picture.

My cat has four legs.

Moja mačka ima četiri noge.

The number "four" is counting to four.

Broj "četiri" broji se na četiri.

Name

I Can...

- [ ] read the 1st sentence.
- [ ] read the 2nd sentence.
- [ ] make a sentence from a picture.
- [ ] color a picture.
- [ ] Draw a picture.

A butterfly has six legs.

Leptir ima šest nogu.

The number "six" is saying 1+5=6.

Broj "šest" govori 1 + 5 = 6.

Name

I Can...

- [ ] read the 1st sentence.
- [ ] read the 2nd sentence.
- [ ] make a sentence from a picture.
- [ ] color a picture.
- [ ] Draw a picture.

A spider has eight legs.

Pauk ima osam nogu.

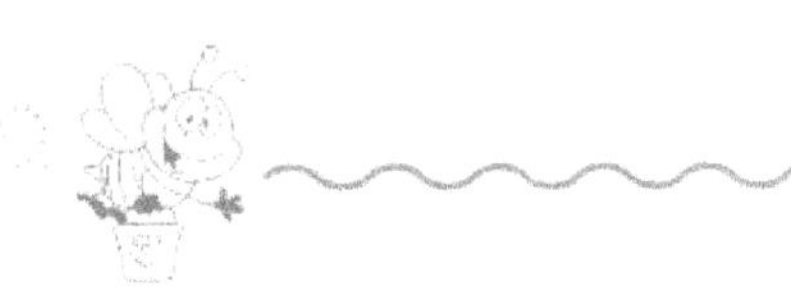

The happy and excited eight is holding up eight fingers

Vesela i uzbuđena osam drži osam prstiju

Name 

I Can...

- [ ] read the 1st sentence.
- [ ] read the 2nd sentence.
- [ ] make a sentence from a picture.
- [ ] color a picture.
- [ ] Draw a picture.

The rooster is going to wake people up.

Pijetao će probuditi ljude.

The rooster is on the fence.

Pijetao je na ogradi.

Name

I Can...

- [ ] read the 1st sentence.
- [ ] read the 2nd sentence.
- [ ] make a sentence from a picture.
- [ ] color a picture.
- [ ] Draw a picture.

My sister has nine stuffed animals.

Moja sestra ima devet napučenih životinja.

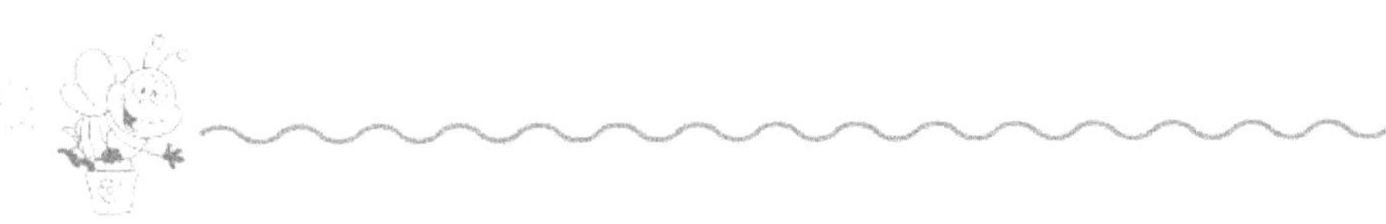

The smiling number nine is saying its name out loud.

Nasmiješeni broj devet izgovara svoje ime naglas.

Name

I Can...

- read the 1st sentence.
- read the 2nd sentence.
- make a sentence from a picture.
- color a picture.
- Draw a picture.

The baby bee has yellow and black stripes.

Dječja pčela ima žute i crne pruge.

The bee is wearing a pink pacifier to calm itself.

Pčela nosi ružičasti piling za smirenje.

Name

I Can...

- [ ] read the 1st sentence.
- [ ] read the 2nd sentence.
- [ ] make a sentence from a picture.
- [ ] color a picture.
- [ ] Draw a picture.

The ladybug has many spots.

Damak ima mnogo spotova.

The red and black ladybug is just done eating some leaves.

Crvena i crna bubica upravo jedu lišće.

Name ___________

I Can...

- [ ] read the 1st sentence.
- [ ] read the 2nd sentence.
- [ ] make a sentence from a picture.
- [ ] color a picture.
- [ ] Draw a picture.

The sheep are skinny.

Ovce su mršave.

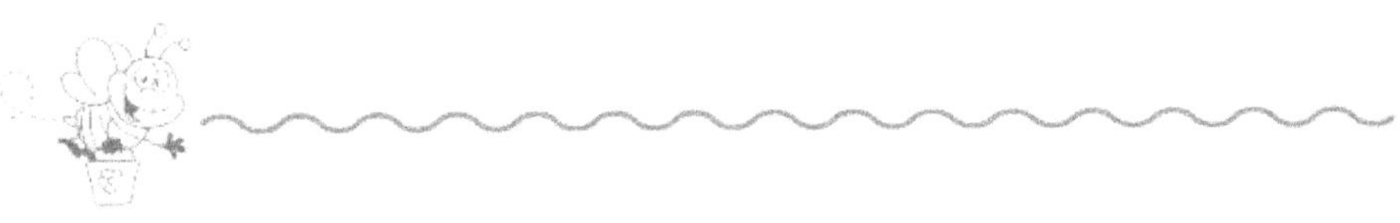

The white sheep have a lot of fluffy white wool to give away.

Bijele ovce imaju puno lepršave bijele vune koju mogu dati.

Name

I Can...

- ☐ read the 1st sentence.
- ☐ read the 2nd sentence.
- ☐ make a sentence from a picture.
- ☐ color a picture.
- ☐ Draw a picture.

The rabbit is entering an egg painting contest.

Zec ulazi na natječaj za slikanje jaja.

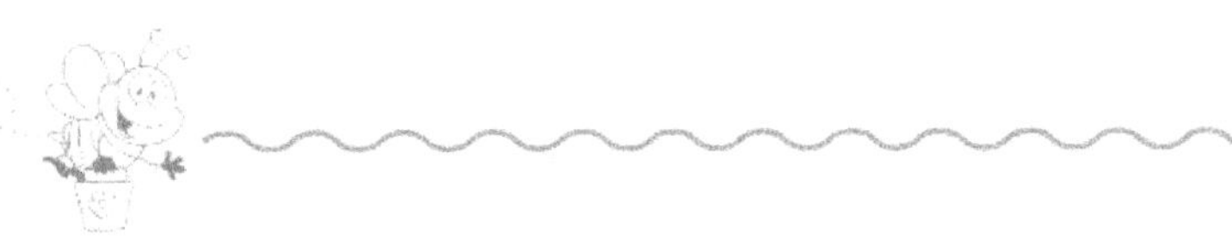

The Easter Bunny is painting a chocolate egg.

Uskršnji zec slika čokoladno jaje.

Name

I Can...

- [ ] read the 1st sentence.
- [ ] read the 2nd sentence.
- [ ] make a sentence from a picture.
- [ ] color a picture.
- [ ] Draw a picture.

The owl is a language arts teacher.

Sova je učiteljica umjetnosti jezika.

An owl is teaching the kids in school about work.

Sova uči djecu u školi o radu.

Name

I Can...

- [ ] read the 1st sentence.
- [ ] read the 2nd sentence.
- [ ] make a sentence from a picture.
- [ ] color a picture.
- [ ] Draw a picture.

The man has an ancient hammer.

Čovjek ima drevni **čekić**.

The builder man has gone to work on a project.

Čovjek graditelj krenuo je raditi na nekom projektu.

Name ___________

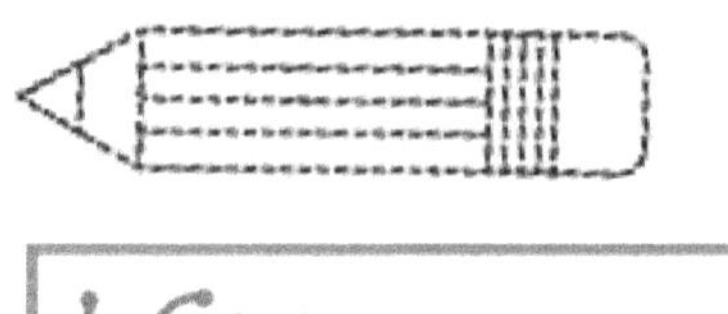

I Can...

- [ ] read the 1st sentence.
- [ ] read the 2nd sentence.
- [ ] make a sentence from a picture.
- [ ] color a picture.
- [ ] Draw a picture.

The goat has a friend.

Koza ima prijatelja.

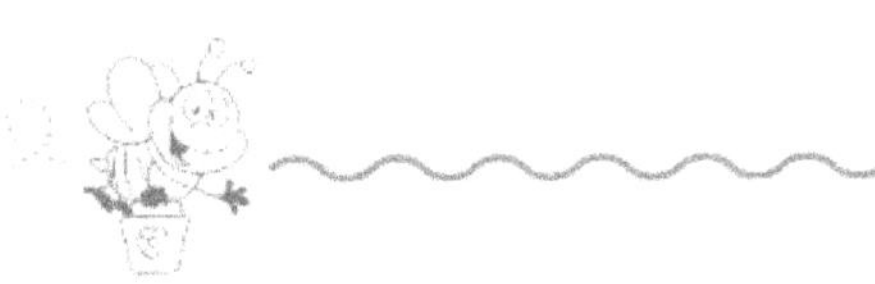

The old goat is proud of its golden bell.

Stara koza ponosna je na svoje zlatno zvono.

Name

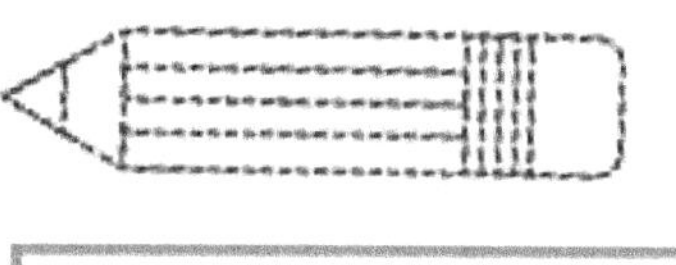

I Can...

- [ ] read the 1st sentence.
- [ ] read the 2nd sentence.
- [ ] make a sentence from a picture.
- [ ] color a picture.
- [ ] Draw a picture.

My mom's friend is a maid.

Prijateljica moje mame je sobarica.

The maid is going to clean the hotel room.

Sluškinja će očistiti hotelsku sobu.

Name

I Can...

- [ ] read the 1st sentence.
- [ ] read the 2nd sentence.
- [ ] make a sentence from a picture.
- [ ] color a picture.
- [ ] Draw a picture.

I went to the zoo.

Otišao sam u zoološki vrt.

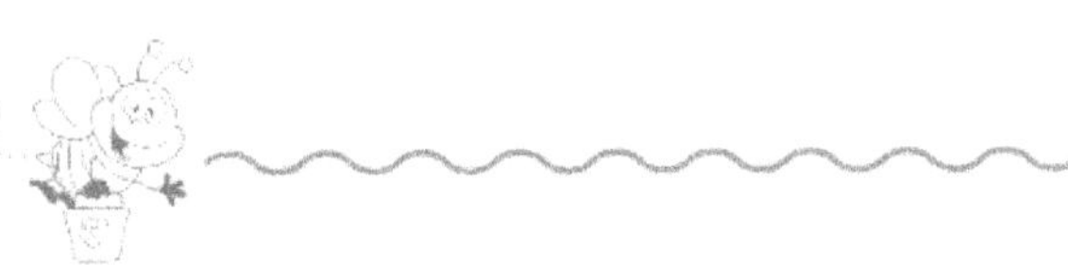

The animals are having a big celebration.

Životinje imaju veliko slavlje.

Name

I Can...

- ☐ read the 1st sentence.
- ☐ read the 2nd sentence.
- ☐ make a sentence from a picture.
- ☐ color a picture.
- ☐ Draw a picture.

The dinosaur has a pillow.

Dinosaur ima jastuk.

The dragon is using the rock to build its house.

Zmaj koristi stijenu za izgradnju svoje kuće.

Name

I Can...

- [ ] read the 1st sentence.
- [ ] read the 2nd sentence.
- [ ] make a sentence from a picture.
- [ ] color a picture.
- [ ] Draw a picture.

The boy is excited to go to school.

Dječak je uzbuđen što ide u školu.

The boy is late for school, so he is sprinting.

Dječak kasni u školu, pa se sprinta.

Name

I Can...

- [ ] read the 1st sentence.
- [ ] read the 2nd sentence.
- [ ] make a sentence from a picture.
- [ ] color a picture.
- [ ] Draw a picture.

The kids on the school bus are going to school.

Djeca u školskom autobusu idu u školu.

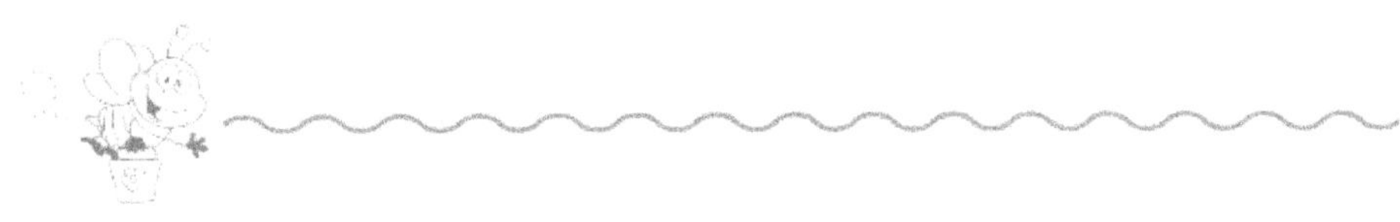

The children are going on a field trip on the yellow bus.

Djeca idu u terenski izlet žutim autobusom.

Name

I Can...

- [ ] read the 1st sentence.
- [ ] read the 2nd sentence.
- [ ] make a sentence from a picture.
- [ ] color a picture.
- [ ] Draw a picture.

The cobra is very lovely.

Kobra je jako draga.

The rattlesnake is looking for its dinner.

Zmijolika traga za svojom večerom.

Name

I Can...

- [ ] read the 1st sentence.
- [ ] read the 2nd sentence.
- [ ] make a sentence from a picture.
- [ ] color a picture.
- [ ] Draw a picture.

That is a fat dog!

To je debeli pas!

This dog is wagging its tail for more treats.

Ovaj pas maše repom radi više poslastica.

Name

I Can...

- ☐ read the 1st sentence.
- ☐ read the 2nd sentence.
- ☐ make a sentence from a picture.
- ☐ color a picture.
- ☐ Draw a picture.

The elephant lives in the zoo.

Slon živi u zoološkom vrtu.

The elephant has a long trunk to spray water.

Slon ima dugo deblo za prskanje vode.

Name

I Can...

- [ ] read the 1st sentence.
- [ ] read the 2nd sentence.
- [ ] make a sentence from a picture.
- [ ] color a picture.
- [ ] Draw a picture.

The giraffe eats vegetables.

Žirafa jede povrće.

The giraffe has an extremely long neck.

Žirafa ima izuzetno dug vrat.

Name

I Can...

- ☐ read the 1st sentence.
- ☐ read the 2nd sentence.
- ☐ make a sentence from a picture.
- ☐ color a picture.
- ☐ Draw a picture.

The chipmunk has a soft tummy.

Čičica ima mekani trbuščić.

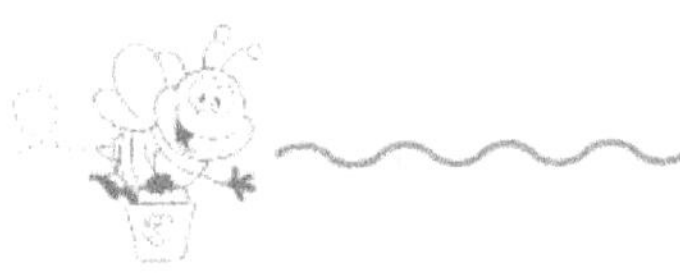

The Chipmunk is about to eat a brown acorn.

Chipmunk će uskoro pojesti smeđu žeđ.

Name

I Can...

- [ ] read the 1st sentence.
- [ ] read the 2nd sentence.
- [ ] make a sentence from a picture.
- [ ] color a picture.
- [ ] Draw a picture.

I have ten toes in total.

Imam ukupno deset nožnih prstiju.

The one and the zero are holding hands.

Jedna i nula se drže za ruke.

Name 

I Can...

- [ ] read the 1st sentence.
- [ ] read the 2nd sentence.
- [ ] make a sentence from a picture.
- [ ] color a picture.
- [ ] Draw a picture.

The alligator is jumping.

Aligator skače.

The crocodile is excited.

Krokodil je uzbuđen.

Name

I Can...

- [ ] read the 1st sentence.
- [ ] read the 2nd sentence.
- [ ] make a sentence from a picture.
- [ ] color a picture.
- [ ] Draw a picture.

I found an ant.

Našao sam mrav.

The ant is telling a story.

Mrav priča priču.

Name

I Can...

- [ ] read the 1st sentence.
- [ ] read the 2nd sentence.
- [ ] make a sentence from a picture.
- [ ] color a picture.
- [ ] Draw a picture.

The bat sleeps upside down.

Šišmiš spava naopako.

The bat is ready to fly.

Šišmiš je spreman za let.

Name

I Can...

- [ ] read the 1st sentence.
- [ ] read the 2nd sentence.
- [ ] make a sentence from a picture.
- [ ] color a picture.
- [ ] Draw a picture.

The cat is very tired.

Mačka je jako umorna.

The cat is taking a nap.

Mačka spava.

Name

I Can...

- [ ] read the 1st sentence.
- [ ] read the 2nd sentence.
- [ ] make a sentence from a picture.
- [ ] color a picture.
- [ ] Draw a picture.

The dog likes to play.

Pas se voli igrati.

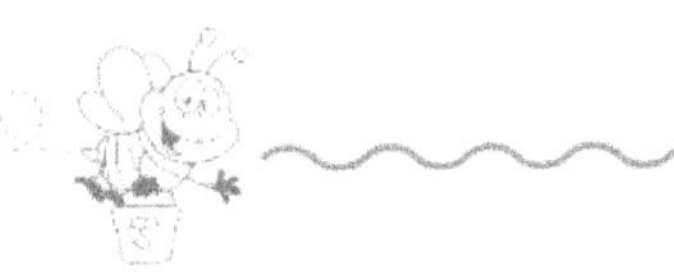

The dog is playing with a bone.

Pas se igra s kostima.

I Can...

- [ ] read the 1st sentence.
- [ ] read the 2nd sentence.
- [ ] make a sentence from a picture.
- [ ] color a picture.
- [ ] Draw a picture.

The elephant has eyelashes.

Slon ima trepavice.

The elephant is shy.

Slon je stidljiv.

Name

I Can...

- [ ] read the 1st sentence.
- [ ] read the 2nd sentence.
- [ ] make a sentence from a picture.
- [ ] color a picture.
- [ ] Draw a picture.

The frog is hopping.

Žaba skače.

The frog is trying to catch the fly.

Žaba pokušava uhvatiti muhu.

Name

I Can...

- [ ] read the 1st sentence.
- [ ] read the 2nd sentence.
- [ ] make a sentence from a picture.
- [ ] color a picture.
- [ ] Draw a picture.

The goat is sleepily walking around.

Koza uspavano hoda uokolo.

The goat is eating grass.

Koza jede travu.

Name

I Can...

- [ ] read the 1st sentence.
- [ ] read the 2nd sentence.
- [ ] make a sentence from a picture.
- [ ] color a picture.
- [ ] Draw a picture.

The hippo has a big head.

Pogon ima veliku glavu.

The hippo has a big head.

Pogon ima veliku glavu.

Name

I Can...

- [ ] read the 1st sentence.
- [ ] read the 2nd sentence.
- [ ] make a sentence from a picture.
- [ ] color a picture.
- [ ] Draw a picture.

The iguana has a long tail.

Iguana ima dugačak rep.

The iguana is hiding behind the letter I.

Iguana se krije iza slova I.

Name

I Can...

- [ ] read the 1st sentence.
- [ ] read the 2nd sentence.
- [ ] make a sentence from a picture.
- [ ] color a picture.
- [ ] Draw a picture.

Mom bought a new bottle of jam.

Mama je kupila novu bocu džema.

There is jam on the bread.

Na kruhu se nalazi džem.

Name

I Can...

- [ ] read the 1st sentence.
- [ ] read the 2nd sentence.
- [ ] make a sentence from a picture.
- [ ] color a picture.
- [ ] Draw a picture.

The kite has a beautiful tail.

Kite imaju prekrasan rep.

The kite is on the ground.

Kite su na zemlji.

Name

I Can...

- [ ] read the 1st sentence.
- [ ] read the 2nd sentence.
- [ ] make a sentence from a picture.
- [ ] color a picture.
- [ ] Draw a picture.

The lion is timid.

Lav je plah.

____

The lion is big.

Lav je velik.

Name

I Can...

- [ ] read the 1st sentence.
- [ ] read the 2nd sentence.
- [ ] make a sentence from a picture.
- [ ] color a picture.
- [ ] Draw a picture.

I like mice.

Volim miševe.

A rat is on top of the letter M

Na vrhu slova M nalazi se štakor

Name

I Can...

- [ ] read the 1st sentence.
- [ ] read the 2nd sentence.
- [ ] make a sentence from a picture.
- [ ] color a picture.
- [ ] Draw a picture.

The nose is breathing.

Nos diše.

The letter N stands for a nose.

Slovo N znači nos.

Name

I Can...

- [ ] read the 1st sentence.
- [ ] read the 2nd sentence.
- [ ] make a sentence from a picture.
- [ ] color a picture.
- [ ] Draw a picture.

The octopus lives underwater.

Hobotnica živi pod vodom.

The octopus has eight tentacles.

Hobotnica ima osam ticala.

Name

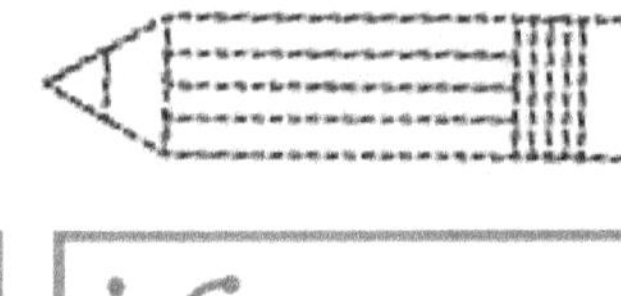

I Can...

- ☐ read the 1st sentence.
- ☐ read the 2nd sentence.
- ☐ make a sentence from a picture.
- ☐ color a picture.
- ☐ Draw a picture.

The penguin eats fish.

Pingvin jede ribu.

The penguin lives in the arctic.

Pingvin živi na Arktiku.

Name

I Can...

- [ ] read the 1st sentence.
- [ ] read the 2nd sentence.
- [ ] make a sentence from a picture.
- [ ] color a picture.
- [ ] Draw a picture.

The queen has a wand.

Kraljica ima štapić.

The queen is beautiful.

Kraljica je lijepa.

Name

I Can...

- [ ] read the 1st sentence.
- [ ] read the 2nd sentence.
- [ ] make a sentence from a picture.
- [ ] color a picture.
- [ ] Draw a picture.

The rabbit has long ears.

Zec ima duge uši.

The rabbit is thinking about something.

Zec razmišlja o nečemu.

Name

I Can...

- [ ] read the 1st sentence.
- [ ] read the 2nd sentence.
- [ ] make a sentence from a picture.
- [ ] color a picture.
- [ ] Draw a picture.

The snake has polka dots.

Zmija ima točkice polke.

The snake is licking its lip because it is hungry.

Zmija liže usne jer je gladna.

Name

I Can...

- [ ] read the 1st sentence.
- [ ] read the 2nd sentence.
- [ ] make a sentence from a picture.
- [ ] color a picture.
- [ ] Draw a picture.

The tortoise has a pointy shell.

Kornjača ima šiljastu školjku.

The turtle has a robust shell but is very slow.

Kornjača ima robusnu školjku, ali je vrlo spora.

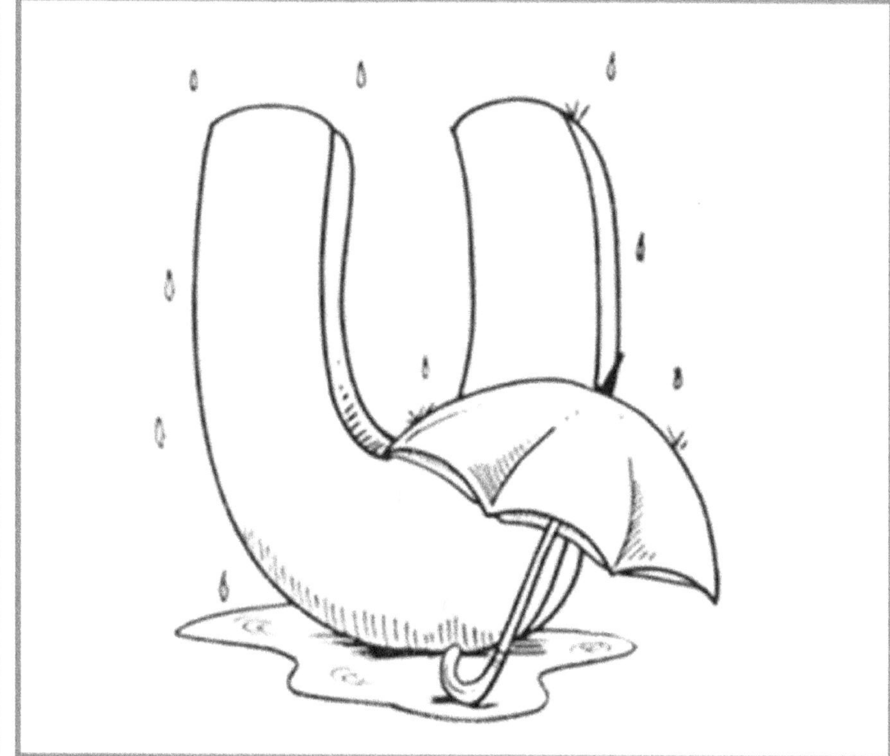

I Can...

- [ ] read the 1st sentence.
- [ ] read the 2nd sentence.
- [ ] make a sentence from a picture.
- [ ] color a picture.
- [ ] Draw a picture.

It's raining.

Pada kiša.

We use the umbrella when it's raining.

Kišobran koristimo kada pada kiša.

Name

I Can...

- ☐ read the 1st sentence.
- ☐ read the 2nd sentence.
- ☐ make a sentence from a picture.
- ☐ color a picture.
- ☐ Draw a picture.

The violin is a musical instrument.

Violina je glazbeni instrument.

A violin can play beautiful music if played correctly.

Violina može svirati prekrasnu glazbu ako se pravilno svira.

Name

I Can...

- [ ] read the 1st sentence.
- [ ] read the 2nd sentence.
- [ ] make a sentence from a picture.
- [ ] color a picture.
- [ ] Draw a picture.

The walrus has a friend.

Morž ima prijatelja.

The walrus has unusually sharp teeth.

Mrtnjak ima neobično oštre zube.

Name

I Can...

- [ ] read the 1st sentence.
- [ ] read the 2nd sentence.
- [ ] make a sentence from a picture.
- [ ] color a picture.
- [ ] Draw a picture.

The xylophone is a colorful instrument.

Ksilofon je šareni instrument.

The xylophone is an instrument like the piano.

Ksilofon je instrument poput klavira.

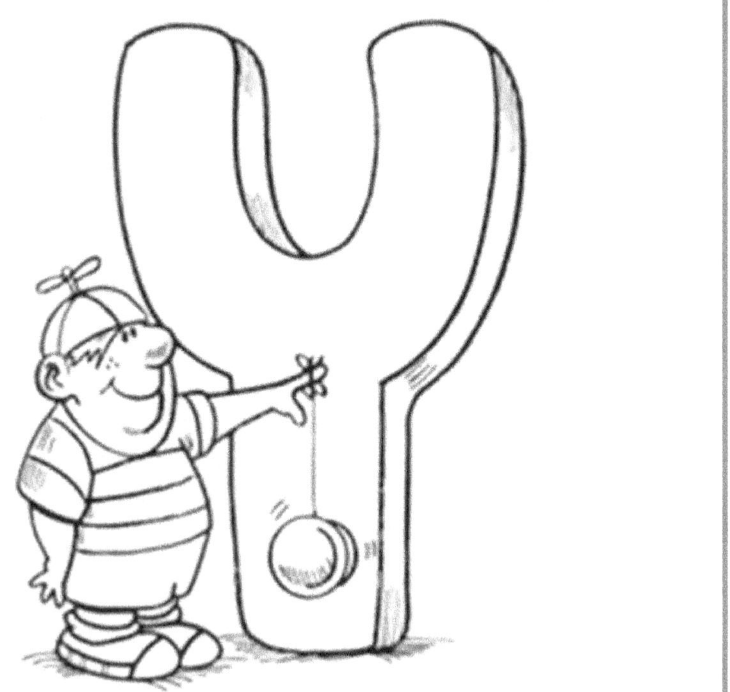

I Can...

- [ ] read the 1st sentence.
- [ ] read the 2nd sentence.
- [ ] make a sentence from a picture.
- [ ] color a picture.
- [ ] Draw a picture.

The boy has a little hat.

Dječak ima mali šešir.

The boy is having fun playing with a yoyo.

Dječak se zabavlja igrajući se s yoyo.

I Can...

- [ ] read the 1st sentence.
- [ ] read the 2nd sentence.
- [ ] make a sentence from a picture.
- [ ] color a picture.
- [ ] Draw a picture.

The zebra has a tail.

Zebra ima rep.

The zebra has black and white stripes.

Zebra ima crne i bijele pruge.

Name

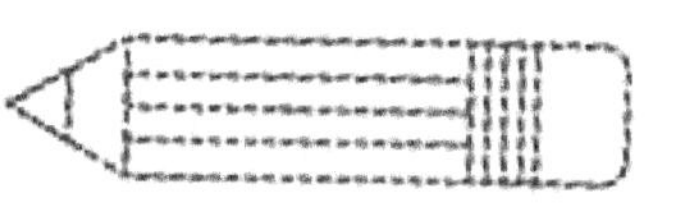

I Can...

- [ ] read the 1st sentence.
- [ ] read the 2nd sentence.
- [ ] make a sentence from a picture.
- [ ] color a picture.
- [ ] Draw a picture.

I have a candle on my cake.

Na torti imam svijeću.

I had a small birthday cake for my party.

Imala sam malu rođendansku tortu za svoju zabavu.

Name ____________________

I Can...

- [ ] read the 1st sentence.
- [ ] read the 2nd sentence.
- [ ] make a sentence from a picture.
- [ ] color a picture.
- [ ] Draw a picture.

The astronaut is going on a mission.

Astronaut ide na misiju.

An astronaut has to explore our universe so that we would have more knowledge.

Astronaut mora istražiti naš svemir kako bismo imali više znanja.

Name _______________

I Can...

- [ ] read the 1st sentence.
- [ ] read the 2nd sentence.
- [ ] make a sentence from a picture.
- [ ] color a picture.
- [ ] Draw a picture.

The samurai is going for a morning jog.

Samuraji idu na jutarnju trku.

The samurai is training to become good at fighting.

Samuraji treniraju kako bi postali dobri u borbi.

Name

I Can...

- [ ] read the 1st sentence.
- [ ] read the 2nd sentence.
- [ ] make a sentence from a picture.
- [ ] color a picture.
- [ ] Draw a picture.

My friend is having a gigantic cake.

Moj prijatelj je gigantski kolač.

I had a humongous birthday cake for my celebration.

Imala sam duhovit rođendanski kolač za svoje slavlje.

Name

I Can...

- [ ] read the 1st sentence.
- [ ] read the 2nd sentence.
- [ ] make a sentence from a picture.
- [ ] color a picture.
- [ ] Draw a picture.

The frog is chasing the fly.

Žaba progoni muhu.

____

The green frog is trying to catch the fly.

Zelena žaba pokušava uhvatiti muhu.

Name

I Can...

- [ ] read the 1st sentence.
- [ ] read the 2nd sentence.
- [ ] make a sentence from a picture.
- [ ] color a picture.
- [ ] Draw a picture.

The ladybug has six legs.

Damak ima šest nogu.

The ladybug is on the leaf.

Damac je na lišću.

Name

I Can...

- [ ] read the 1st sentence.
- [ ] read the 2nd sentence.
- [ ] make a sentence from a picture.
- [ ] color a picture.
- [ ] Draw a picture.

The dragon is sick.

Zmaj je bolestan.

The dragon just ate something spicy, so he needed water.

Zmaj je samo pojeo nešto začinjeno, pa mu je trebala voda.

Name

I Can...

- ☐ read the 1st sentence.
- ☐ read the 2nd sentence.
- ☐ make a sentence from a picture.
- ☐ color a picture.
- ☐ Draw a picture.

That is a baby cow.

To je beba krava.

A little cow is walking around near the barn.

Mala krava hoda okolo u blizini staje.

I Can...

- [ ] read the 1st sentence.
- [ ] read the 2nd sentence.
- [ ] make a sentence from a picture.
- [ ] color a picture.
- [ ] Draw a picture.

The frog has a big smile.

Žaba ima veliki osmijeh.

The frog is smiling because it is happy.

Žaba se smiješi jer je sretna.

Name

I Can...

- ☐ read the 1st sentence.
- ☐ read the 2nd sentence.
- ☐ make a sentence from a picture.
- ☐ color a picture.
- ☐ Draw a picture.

The frog has a big mouth.

Žaba ima velika usta.

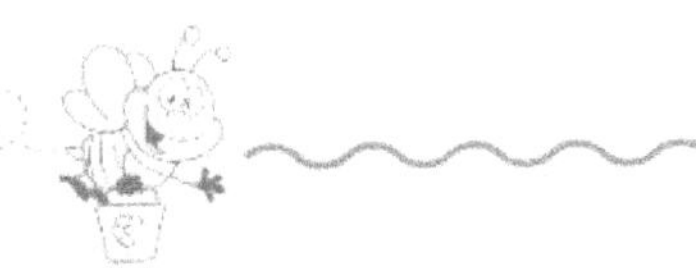

The frog is waving to us.

Žaba nam maše.